Design and History

The design of the Imperial Japanese Navy (IJN) *Kongo* class battle-cruisers originated from Great Britain. At first the new warships were to follow the Royal Navy (RN) *Invincible* class, but, impressed with the new RN *Lion* class, the IJN opted for an improved version of that design.

The lead ship of this then new class of battlecruiser, *Kongo*, was built at the Vickers & Sons Shipyard in Great Britain. However, at that time Japan was quickly expanding its ship building capabilities, and set out to construct the remaining three vessels of the class in Japan. For the *Hiei*, approximately 30% of construction material was supplied from England, but *Kirishima* and *Haruna* were constructed entirely with material from Japan. All machinery and armament for *Hiei*, *Kirishima* and *Haruna* was fabricated in Japan under licence.

As originally designed, the *Kongo*s were battlecruisers, requiring high speeds, necessitating a massive steam plant of 36 coal fired boilers. On trial, *Kongo* attained nearly 28 knots. *Kongo* also had the feature of oil spaying, which meant that oil could be sprayed onto the coal fires for a small increase in range and power.

Soon after the completion of all four of the *Kongo* class battlecruisers, they each had minor up-grades to the bridge structures. During the 'Great War' life for the *Kongo* class was largely uneventful, except for *Haruna*. She hit what was believed to be

■ *KONGO* CLASS BATTLECRUISERS: GENERAL STATISTICS AS BUILT, 1913-15

Displacement:	32,200 tons
Dimensions:	Length 704ft, Beam 92ft, Draft 27.5ft
Armament:	8 – 14in/45cal, 16 – 6in/50cal, 8 – 3.1in AA, 8 – 21 TT
Armour:	Belt 8in, Deck 2.5in, Barbettes 10in, Turrets 9in face, 2in roof
Machinery:	36 Coal Fired Boilers, 4 Parsons Turbines @ 64,000shp
Range:	9500nm @ 14kts
Top Speed:	27.5kts

Kongo on sea trials off the coast of England, shortly after her fitting out period was completed at the Vickers & Sons Shipyard, Barrow.

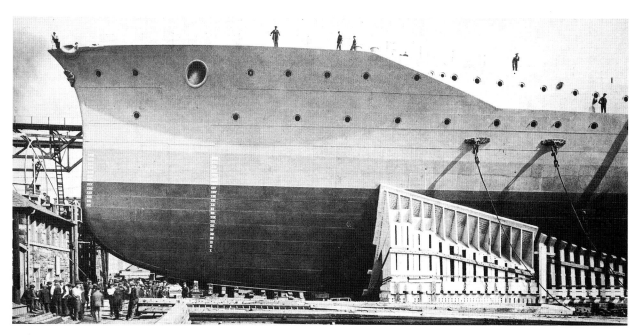

A view of the bow of *Kongo* just prior to her launching. Note the unique shape of her forefoot.

Kongo, again just prior to her launching at the Vickers & Sons Shipyard, Barrow. Her massive propellers are visible in this image.

a German mine in the summer of 1917. She nearly sank from the extensive flooding, but just managed to make port for repairs. By 1918, the 3in AA mounts were removed from atop the main gun turrets. In the early 1920s, an odd shaped cowling was added to the fore funnel to keep smoke away from the back of the bridge structure on all vessels of the class.

By the late 1920s, a major reconstruction of the four *Kongo*s was planned, as Japan was still adhering to the Washington Naval Treaty. *Haruna* was first to enter Yokosuka dockyard in March 1924, *Kirishima* at Kure in March 1927, both *Kongo* at Yokosuka and *Hiei* at Kure in September 1929. *Kongo*, *Kirishima* and *Haruna* would each receive additional armour protection, more efficient oil fired boilers, reduction to two funnels, main gun elevation raised to 43°, aircraft facilities between main gun turrets 3 and 4, and anti-torpedo bulges on the hull. *Hiei* was demilitarised at this time, with removal of side armour, No 4 main gun turret, all 6in broadside guns removed and a reduction of boilers to reduce her top speed to 18kts. *Haruna* completed this major reconstruction in July 1928, *Kirishima* in March 1930, *Kongo* in March 1931 and *Hiei* completed her demilitarisation in December 1932. Due to the increase in both weight and beam, the top speed of the first three fell 2.5kts. and it was at this time that these warships were re-rated as battleships.

During the early 1930s, the *Kongo* class battleships had a few modifications, including the addition of 150cm search-

■ *KONGO* CLASS BATTLECRUISERS:
FIRST MAJOR RECONSTRUCTION, 1927-32

Displacement:	34,400 tons
Dimensions:	Length 704ft, Beam 102ft, Draft 28.3ft
Armament:	8 – 14in/45cal, 16 – 6in/50cal, 8 – 3.1in AA, 4 – 21 TT
Armour:	Belt 8in, Deck 4.7in, Barbettes 13in, Turrets 9in face, 5in roof
Machinery:	10 Oil & Coal Fired Boilers, 4 Parsons Turbines @ 64,000shp
Range:	8900nm @ 14kts
Top Speed:	26kts

HIJMS *Kongo* about to depart English waters with her Japanese crew. She was commissioned into the Imperial Japanese Navy at that time.

lights for improved night fighting, four pairs of twin 127mm AA mounts, twin 40mm AA mounts, quadruple 13mm AA mounts, mainmast reduced in height and a catapult added to the aircraft deck between turrets 3 and 4. This was accomplished on a ship by ship basis, as time allowed.

Even as work was finished on these vessels, another major reconstruction was drawn up for the *Kongo* class battleships. *Haruna* went into the Kure Navy Yard in August 1933, *Kirishima* at Sasebo in June 1934, *Kongo* at Yokosuka in June 1935. This would be the most extensive of all reconstructions done to the *Kongo*s. They had their stern lengthened by 25ft and all boilers were replaced with more efficient oil fired units, giving these vessels an increase in speed to 30kts. An upgraded catapult and expansion of the aircraft handling deck, improved barbette armour, and removal of the foremost 6in casemate guns

HIJMS *Hiei* in a drydock on 15 March 1915, during the Great War, at which time the Japanese were part of the Allied Forces.

Haruna, fitting out in October 1914.

Kirishima soon after commissioning, taken 21 December 1915. Note the anti-torpedo net booms and shelving, but no nets at that date.

were other improvements. The entire bridge structure was radically rebuilt, enlarging all the platforms substantially, as well as adding searchlight towers around the fore funnel. A large after fire control tower was constructed abaft the mainmast with duplicate systems to those atop the bridge. The then new twin 25mm AA mounts were also installed at this time. *Haruna* completed in September 1934, followed by *Kirishima* in June 1936 and *Kongo* in January 1937.

Japan rejected the Washington Naval Treaty in 1936 and in doing so, drew up plans to reconstruct *Hiei*. All components removed earlier had been carefully stored and were then reused where needed. *Hiei* had the same modifications as her sisterships during this reconstruction, but the bridge structure was built to a new experi-

mental design, and her armour was also improved over that of her sisterships. Her reconstruction began in November 1936 at Kure and was completed by December 1939.

By the early 1940s, the *Kongo*s had minor improvements to the bridge in the form of an air defence platform at the top level, as well as additional flash protection to the main turrets. In 1941, a degaussing cable was fitted to the exterior of the hull at the deck edge on all four vessels of this class. By the middle of 1941, the *Kongo* class battleships would then have all the latest technology available from the Imperial Japanese Navy.

By August 1941, all four of the *Kongo*s were stationed together with the First Fleet, at the Combined Fleet anchorage

Hiroshima Bay, making up Battleship Division 3 (BatDiv3). *Hiei* and *Kirishima* made up Section 1 and *Kongo* and *Haruna* Section 2.

In November 1941, BatDiv3, Section 1 joined First Fleet Striking Force at Hitokappu Bay, while BatDiv3, Section 2 joined Second Fleet Southern Force at Mako, Pescadores Islands.

In December 1941, *Hiei* and *Kirishima* (BatDiv3/1) were the primary escort for the surprise attack upon the US Navy at Pearl Harbor, Hawaii. They returned to Hitokappu Bay by the end of that month. *Kongo* and *Haruna* (BatDiv3/2) were the

primary escort for the invasion of Indochina. They deployed to intercept the British 'Force Z', *Prince of Wales* and *Repulse*, but the British force was sunk by IJN land based bombers before interception could take place. BatDiv3/2 returned to Mako by early January 1942.

BatDiv3/1 moved to the new primary IJN anchorage at Truk Lagoon in January 1942. BatDiv3/2 was the cover force for the Japanese Invasion of the Dutch East Indies during the same month.

During February and March 1942, BatDiv3/1 escorted the Carrier Striking Force during raids on Port Darwin,

A view on board the collier *Kaga Maru*, while supplying *Haruna*. Note the unique camouflage painting of *Haruna*.

Another view of *Haruna* with her unique camouflage, taken in October 1915. It is believed that this was an anti-submarine deception pattern.

Kirishima's bridge structure, 4 May 1922.

Australia, and the Battle of the Java Sea, returning to Staring Bay anchorage. BatDiv3/2 escorted the force that invaded the Netherlands East Indies, then bombarded Christmas Island, before returning to Staring Bay.

April 1942 saw the entire *Kongo* class battleships operate together as the escort for the Carrier Striking Force on a raid into the Indian Ocean against the British Royal Navy. They retired to the newly captured IJN base at Singapore by mid-April to refuel. The majority of the Striking Force

and BatDiv3 then steamed to Japan, arriving at the end of April.

May 1942 saw the transfer of *Kongo* to BatDiv3, Section 1, then made up of *Kongo* and *Hiei*, with BatDiv3/2 then made up of *Haruna* and *Kirishima*. Both *Kongo* and *Haruna* had minor refits that month as well. At the end of that month, BatDiv3/1 escorted the Main Body of the Japanese Fleet, while BatDiv3/2 escorted the Carrier Strike Force to the Battle of Midway on June 4-6. *Haruna* was slightly damaged by USN carrier air attack, but at the end of the

■ *KONGO* CLASS BATTLECRUISERS: SECOND MAJOR RECONSTRUCTION, 1933-40

Displacement:	36,600 tons
Dimensions:	Length 729ft, Beam 102ft, Draft 31.5ft
Armament:	8 – 14in/45cal, 14 – 6in/50cal, 8 – 5in AA, 10 – 25mm AA
Armour:	Belt 8in, Deck 4.7in, Barbettes 13.5in, Turrets 9in face, 5in roof
Machinery:	8 Oil Fired Boilers, 4 Parsons Turbines @ 136,000shp
Range:	10,000nm @ 14kts
Top Speed:	30.5kts

battle she and *Kirishima* picked up survivors from the sunken carriers. All of BatDiv3 returned to Japan by mid-June.

In July, BatDiv3 was consolidated to *Kongo* and *Haruna*, while *Kirishima* and *Hiei* made up the then new BatDiv11. All four *Kongos* had a minor refit, and *Kongo* was fitted with Type 21 Air and Surface Search Radar, through to mid-August.

During the period of mid-August through mid-September, all four *Kongo* class battleships participated in battle practice in Japanese waters. Afterwards, all four *Kongos* departed from Japan, BatDiv3, made up of *Kongo* and *Haruna*, and BatDiv11's *Kirishima* and *Hiei*, arrived at Truk. From there they departed for the Solomon Islands, BatDiv3 with cruisers in the Bombardment Force and BatDiv11 escorting the Carrier Strike Force. The operation was cancelled, and the entire force returned to Truk by late September.

Above: Midships area of *Kongo* during 1927. Note the unique shape of the cap on her forward funnel, designed to deflect smoke away from the superstructure.

Below: *Hiei* during battle maneuvers at sea.

Midships view of *Haruna*, 28 May 1928, while on post-refit trials at the conclusion of her first major reconstruction.

Midships view of *Kirishima*, taken about 1931. She has had a reduction in the number of funnels to two, a result of her re-boilering in 1927.

At that time *Kongo* and *Haruna* were fitted with the Type 22 Surface Search Radar.

By Mid-October 1942, both BatDiv3 and 11 departed again for the Solomon Islands. *Kongo* and *Haruna* bombarded Henderson Field on Guadalcanal Island on the night of October 13. The Battle of Santa Cruz took place on 25-26 October, where BatDiv3 and 11 covered the IJN Carrier Strike Force, with BatDiv11 attacked numerous times, but not hit. The IJN Fleet returned to Truk at the end of October. After refuelling BatDiv11 transferred to Shortland Island.

Kirishima and *Hiei*, as BatDiv11, steamed for Guadalcanal, arriving 13 November, to be deployed as the bombardment force for an invasion of that island. At 0150 hrs the Japanese force of BatDiv11, with light cruiser *Nagara* and 13 destroyers, opened fire upon the US Navy cruisers and destroyers around Savo Island. The first Battle of Guadalcanal, also known as the 'Bar Room Brawl', was a very confusing gun and torpedo battle that took place at close quarters in the night. *Kirishima* was hit by only one 8in shell with minimal damage, but *Hiei* was badly damaged by a torpedo hit and as many as

thirty 8in shells, even more 5in and was sprayed by 20mm rounds. By daybreak of 13 November *Hiei* had managed to limp to the west of Savo Island, only to be attacked by numerous USAAF bombers, USN and USMC land and carrier borne aircraft. She was hit numerous times and was last seen, a smoldering wreck, sinking sometime just after midnight on November 14. *Hiei* has the dubious distinction of being the first Imperial Japanese Navy battleship sunk during the Second World War. *Hiei* and *Kirishima* managed to sink the US Navy light cruiser *Atlanta*, four destroyers and severely damage two heavy, two light cruisers and one destroyer.

The second Battle of Guadalcanal began in the very early morning darkness of 15 November, at 0016hrs, as ships of both the IJN and USN manoeuvred south of Savo Island. The USN battleships *South Dakota* and *Washington* with destroyers opened fire upon IJN light cruisers *Nagara*, *Sendai* and destroyers in a sweep towards Guadalcanal. *Kirishima*, heavy cruisers *Atago* and *Takao* fired upon *South Dakota*. *Kirishima* hit the American battleship only once, but the heavy cruisers obtained many

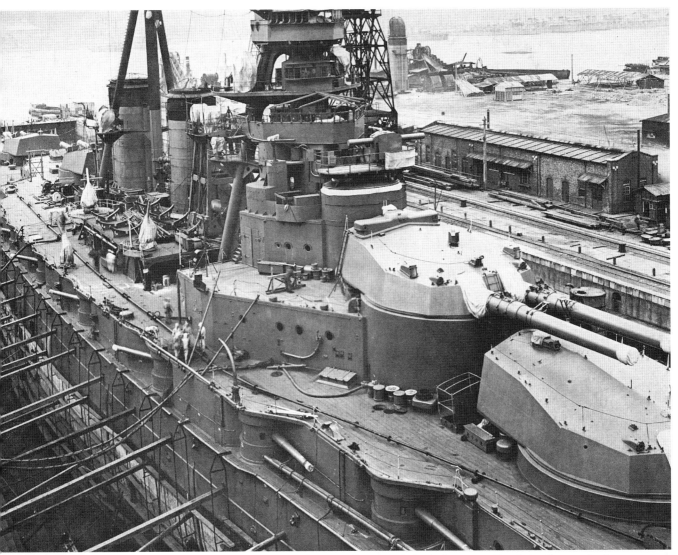

Above: *Kongo* in drydock at Yokosuka Navy Yard, 29 December 1929. She was in the beginning stages of her first major reconstruction.

Below: *Kongo* nearing the conclusion of her first major reconstruction, 20 February 1931.

Above: Two photographs of the bridge structure of *Hiei* from the mid-1930s.

Below: A broadside view of *Hiei* during the mid-1930s as a de-militarised training vessel.

hits. Suddenly, unobserved by the IJN, at 0100hrs, *Washington* fired upon *Kirishima* with main battery 16in guns and *Atago* and *Takao* with secondary battery 5in guns. *Kirishima* was hit by nine 16in shells in less than six minutes, knocking her completely out of action. She had also been hit by as many as forty 5in shells. *Washington* also hit *Atago* and *Takao* several times with 5in shells. *Kirishima*'s rudder was jammed and she steamed in a circle, burning furiously.

She began to list to starboard, and at 0325hrs, capsized seven miles NW of Savo Island. As she capsized, her forward magazines detonated, blasting the battleship in two as she sank.

Kongo and *Haruna* of BatDiv3 escorted the carrier *Junyo* in search of the USN carrier *Enterprise*, but were unsuccessful and by 17 Novemebr 1942 had returned to Truk. BatDiv3 remained at Truk for the rest of that year.

At the end of January 1943, BatDiv3 formed part of a large fleet acting as a diversion so that IJN destroyers could evacuate Japanese Army troops from Guadalcanal. They had returned to Truk by 9 February after a successful operation.

At the end of February, BatDiv3 returned to Japan for an overhaul at the Kure Naval Base. *Haruna* was fitted with the Type 21 Radar system, and both battleships had six 6in secondary guns removed at the same time, as well as additional 25mm mounts

installed. Concrete protection was added around the steering gear. This refit was finished by the end of March 1943.

BatDiv3 steamed for the Truk anchorage by mid-April, only to remain inactive until departing for Yokosuka in mid-May. *Kongo* and *Haruna* remained in Japanese waters until mid-June, before returning to Truk.

In late September 1943, BatDiv3 with other IJN fleet units, steamed to Eniwetok in response to US Navy attacks upon Tarawa, Makin, and Abemama Atolls. With

Above: *Kongo*, in drydock, May 1933. Note the awkward placement of the catapult at that time.

Below: The aircraft deck aboard *Kongo*, 1934.

Above: Both views are of the aircraft handling deck areas aboard a *Kongo* class battleship.

Below: *Haruna* on her post reconstruction trials, September 1934.

Kongo and *Haruna* transferred to Sasebo Naval Base, Japan in mid-December 1943 for drydocking and were fitted with additional 25mm AA mounts. This refit was completed in mid-February 1944, and they then exercised in the Inland Sea until early March.

BatDiv3, still made up of *Kongo* and *Haruna*, in company with other IJN fleet units, steamed for the Lingga anchorage in mid-March 1944. Once there, BatDiv3 trained in Indonesian waters and visited Singapore on one occasion, until transfering to a new anchorage at Tawi Tawi with the majority of IJN fleet from May through mid-June.

BatDiv3 moved to Philippine waters for the Battle of Philippine Sea in mid-June 1944. *Kongo* and *Haruna* were part of Force C, which sortied east through the Philippine Sea toward Saipan. On 20 June they were attacked by aircraft from the USN carriers *Bunker Hill*, *Monterey* and *Cabot*. *Kongo* was not hit, but *Haruna* was struck by 500lb bombs on No 4 turret and the quarterdeck, but managed to maintain top speed. BatDiv3 retired, via Okinawa to refuel and returned to Japan by the end of June.

While at the Kure Naval Base in early July, *Kongo* was drydocked and received additional 25mm AA mounts and Type 13 Radar. *Haruna's* bomb damage was repaired at that time at Sasebo, where she received similar upgrades to those for *Kongo*.

Kongo departed on 8 July for the Lingga anchorage, without *Haruna*, but with other main IJN fleet units. *Haruna* departed Sasebo with destroyers and arrived at Lingga in late August 1944. Both units of BatDiv3 would remain at the Lingga anchorage until mid-October.

BatDiv3 departed Lingga for Brunei Bay, Borneo in late October 1944. From there they sortied with other major units of the IJN fleet, known as Force A, for Leyte Gulf.

no action, the IJN Fleet returned to Truk by the end of September. Again, BatDiv3 sortied from Truk in mid-October in response to a US Navy attack upon Wake Island, but again, the IJN fleet took no action, returning to Truk by the end of October.

This was the beginning of the Battle of Leyte Gulf, a conflict that had smaller clashes within the main battle. As the IJN fleet passed through the Palawan Passage, they were intercepted by the USN submarines *Darter* and *Dace*. These submarines were able to torpedo three heavy cruisers, *Takao*, *Atago* and *Maya*, severely damaging *Takao* and sinking the other two. The rest of the IJN fleet passed without harm. This event was later known as the Battle of Palawan Passage.

The remaining IJN fleet units, including BatDiv3, proceeded into the Sibuyan Sea, where USN carrier aircraft attacked the entire IJN fleet with over 250 aircraft, sinking the super battleship *Musashi*. *Kongo* was not hit, but again, *Haruna* was damaged by near misses.

In the early hours of 25 October 1944,

the IJN fleet surprised a division of USN escort aircraft carriers off Samar Island. In the ensuing melee, the Japanese battle-ships and heavy cruisers, including *Kongo* and *Haruna* fired upon the hapless small carriers, but were run off by USN destroyers in a brave torpedo attack. The IJN sank one carrier, and three destroyers at the cost of three heavy cruisers.

On the following day, USAAF B-24 bombers attack the retiring IJN fleet, hitting the super battleship *Yamato*, sinking the light cruiser *Noshiro*, but *Kongo* and *Haruna* were unharmed. The remnants of Force A arrived at Brunei on 28 October 1944.

In early November, BatDiv3 left Brunei Bay to escort a resupply mission by other warships to Manila for the Japanese Army. They returned to Brunei by mid-November.

Haruna on one of her post reconstruction trials, this one in August 1934.

A broadside view of *Hiei* during 1935, as a de-militarised training vessel.

Above: *Kongo* running high speed trials after her reconstruction on 14 November 1936.

■ *KONGO* CLASS BATTLECRUISERS: WARTIME IMPROVEMENTS, 1941-45

Displacement:	36,600 – 40,200 tons
Dimensions:	Length 729ft, Beam 102ft, Draft 31.5 – 33ft
Armament:	8 – 14in/45cal, 14 to 8 – 6in/50cal, 8 to 12 – 5in AA, 10 to 72 – 25mm AA
	8 – 13mm AA, 30 – Depth Charges
Armour:	Belt 8in, Deck 4.7in, Barbettes 13.5in, Turrets 9in face, 5in roof
Machinery:	8 Oil Fired Boilers, 4 Parsons Turbines @ 136,000shp
Range:	10,000 to 8800nm @ 14kts
Top Speed:	29 to 30.5kts

Below: A close-up view of *Kongo*'s superstructure from the above photograph.

At that time, the battleship *Nagato* was assigned to BatDiv3. On November 16, the IJN fleet at Brunei was attacked by USAAF B-24 bombers and P-38 fighters. *Kongo* and *Haruna* were not damaged. On that same day, *Kongo*, in company with *Yamato*, *Nagato*, light cruiser *Yahagi* and six destroyers departed for Japan. The next day, *Haruna* and the heavy cruisers *Ashigara*, *Haguro* and light cruiser *Oyodo* departed for the Lingga anchorage, via the Spratly Island anchorage.

Meanwhile, on 21 November, in the early morning, *Kongo* and her companions were off of Formosa, making 16kts, when they were intercepted by the USN submarine *Sealion*. At 0256 hrs *Sealion* fired all six bow tubes, turned and fired all four stern tubes by 0300hrs. Minutes later, two huge geysers of water shot up into the air alongside the port side of *Kongo*, which shook with a terrible shudder. Another minute later, one of the destroyers disappeared in a huge explosion, sinking immediately. One torpedo hit forward, at the leading edge of *Kongo*'s torpedo blister, with the other striking her abreast the second funnel, flooding several engine rooms. *Kongo*'s captain kept up her speed, but in so doing caused her damage from the forward hit to worsen and increase flooding, also increasing the warship's list to almost 45°. Soon her speed slowed to 10kts. About 0520, *Kongo* went dead in the water with her list increasing. At 0524, *Kongo* capsized to port, at the same time causing her forward magazine to detonate.

On 22 November *Haruna*, along with the cruisers and destroyers arrived at Lingga. As she was attempting to anchor, she grounded on a reef, doing significant damage to her hull, necessitating repairs in Japan. *Haruna* departed Lingga alone for Singapore on 28 November to pick up two destroyers and continued on to Mako, where she joined the carrier *Junyo* and three destroyers on 5 December 1944. This group departed for Japan the next day.

Below: A broadside view of *Kirishima* about May 1937, Sukumo Bay.

Bottom: A broadside view of *Kongo* about January 1937.

Kirishima off Amoy, China, 21 October 1938, photographed by the American destroyer USS *Pillsbury*.

Right: *Kongo* refueling. The IJN method of underway replenishment was side by side, as with the USN, but also inline, like that of the *Kriegsmarine*.

Close-up of the same image as above of *Kirishima*.

On 9 December en route to Japan, the IJN task group was intercepted by a USN submarine group. The carrier *Junyo* was struck by two torpedoes, as was one of the escorting destroyers. All IJN warships arrived at Sasebo Navy Yard the next day. *Haruna* and two destroyers continued on to Kure the day after, arriving two days later.

Haruna was drydocked and hull damage was repaired. She really needed an extensive refit due to the numerous times she had been damaged, but this was not possible due to the lack of supplies and constant air attacks. Also, because of the lack of fuel available, *Haruna* remained in port, assigned to the Kure Naval District.

On 19 March 1945, USN carriers launched a massive air assault upon the Kure Naval District. *Haruna* was hit once, with slight damage, but June 22 saw another air assault, this time by USAAF B-29s, with one bomb hit on the quarterdeck causing slight damage. On 24 July yet another carrier aircraft attack resulted in three bomb hits and moderate damage.

The end came for *Haruna* on 28 July 1945. This was another carrier aircraft attack, obtaining about nine hits. She sank in very shallow water, her fore and centredeck above water. Her wreck was later broken up between 1946 and 1948.

This, and the other images on this page are colorised black & white photographs, this one showing *Haruna* at speed during her post-refit trials in September 1934.

HIJMS *Hiei* in a drydock in November 1941, just prior to her departure for Hawaiian waters for the Pearl Harbor Operation.

A view over the bow of *Kongo*, running at high speed across a flat sea, 25 February 1942. Note the stuffed canvas rolls, used for splinter protection, as well as rope, seen wrapped around the arm of the director.

This image, and the others are stills pulled from a colour film taken by the US Navy in October 1945 during a survey of the remnants of the Imperial Japanese Navy. *Haruna* was the only one of the four *Kongo*s to survive until the last weeks of hostilities. She is seen here in these images painted in a green camouflage.

In this image, the extent of the bomb damage to *Haruna* is evident. Rust is seen, as the paint was damaged by fire and blast.

This view of the forward turrets shows a camouflage of dark grey stripes diagonally over the green base paint.

Reference Material

GAKKEN 21 – *KONGO* CLASS BATTLESHIPS

This is one of many such volumes in a great series of pictorials of IJN warships. Contained within this book are a good number of photos and drawings of these ships, as well as photographs of some very nice scratch built 1/200 scale models of *Kongo* and *Haruna*. The text is Japanese, but this is still a valuable reference source because of all the visual material contained.

KOJINSHA 2 – *KONGO* CLASS BATTLESHIPS

Volume 2 in another excellent series of pictorials on IJN warships. Contained within this book are a great number of photos and some simplified drawings of these ships. This is a hard bound compilation of the older *Maru* Series soft bound individual books by the same publisher. Again, the text is Japanese, but this is still a valuable reference source because of all the visual material contained.

MODEL ART 15 – *KONGO* CLASS BATTLESHIPS

One of yet another great series of pictorials about modelling IJN warships. Contained within this book are a good number of photos of models and good drawings of these ships. Models in 1/700 are shown through construction to their finish, with conversions to pre-war variants. Information about model accessory kits is also provided. The text is Japanese, but this is still a valuable reference source because of all the visual material contained.

IMPERIAL JAPANESE NAVY GREYS

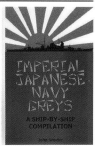

This is a small booklet from a knowledgeable source on the painting of warships, including Japanese. Contained within the pages is information about when and where IJN warships were painted and with which shade of IJN Grey. Also included is information on how to obtain paint samples of the different IJN Greys and Greens. This is a valuable tool for accurately modeling the paint schemes of the IJN.

WARSHIP PICTORIAL 13 – *KONGO* CLASS BATTLESHIPS

The only English language book on the *Kongo*s, containing a large number of photographs and drawings of these warships throughout their existence. Also within this book is a chronological history of each battleship during the Pacific War period. This book is a must have for photographs of this class of IJN warship.

Model Kits

1/2400 SCALE

Above: GHQ 1/2400 HIJMS *Hiei* 1942

This scale is primarily for war gaming. The smallest, 1/2400 are manufactured by GHQ and come unpainted and require some assembly. Their quality is quite good considering their really small size. A *Kongo* class battleship in 1/2400 is only 3.65in in length, making this scale good for table-top naval war gaming.

1/1250 SCALE

This scale is now the new world standard. Its primary use is for war gaming, but the extremely high level of detail has also made these models collectors' items and are great to display. The largest manufacturer is Navis/Neptun of Germany. All World War I and earlier topics are under the Navis name, while the WWII topics and modern subjects are sold under the Navis label. The quality of both is good with the detail on the Navis topics ranging from adequate to great, while the Neptun detail is fantastic.

Above left: Navis Models 1/1250 HIJMS *Kongo* 1914
Left: Neptun Models 1/1250 HIJMS *Kongo* 1942

1/1200 SCALE

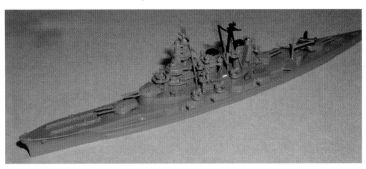

*Kongo*s are found in this scale from Konishi of Japan and Superior of USA. This scale is also used for war gaming. The quality of these models is good, but the detail is basic. They are available from Konishi pre-built and painted, and unpainted from Superior.

Photo by Collin Riley

Above left: Konishi Models 1/1200 HIJMS *Haruna* 1937
Left: Superior Models 1/1200 HIJMS *Haruna* 1937

1/700 SCALE

■ Not surprisingly, the first plastic model kits of the *Kongo* class battleships were manufactured in Japan. Among those initial releases were those from Nichimo. These were in a rather odd '30cm scale', where all warships in this series were 30cm in length. This soon developed into 1/700 scale, which was just a little larger, but retained the same look.

Fujimi of Japan produced the first set of *Kongo* class battleship plastic kits in 1/700 scale. These were the mainstay in this now most popular of all ship modelling scales. Quality was good, but the accuracy suffered noticably. The smaller detail parts were not just over scale but also over simplified. Superstructures were not correct. In fact, the box art was one of the major selling points for these kits because the artwork was very good and rather more accurate. As the years passed, more and more books with photos and drawings of these vessels appeared, providing model builders with the reference to correct these kits. With the advent of photo-etch, detail parts also became available in the late 1980s, helping to improve the accuracy of these kits even further.

In 1993 Hasegawa of Japan produced an all new set of kits of the *Kongo* class battleships that were much more accurate. The level of detail was vastly improved on the hull, superstucture and the detail parts, including weapons, aircraft and fittings, with much better represented superstructures, making these kits a huge improvement over the older Fujimi kits.

Fujimi 1/700 HIJMS *Hiei* 1942

Hasegawa 1/700 HIJMS *Kongo* 1944

Hasegawa 1/700 HIJMS *Haruna* 1944

1/500 SCALE

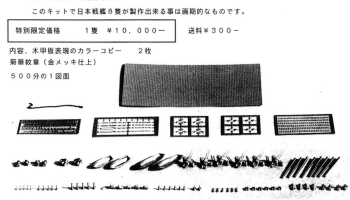

●５００分の１洋上模型キット

『戦艦キット』発売!!

「金剛」キット

このキットで「比叡」「榛名」「霧島」の4隻が出来ますが、砲塔、後檣に変化があり、申

「艦橋」のない戦艦キットの計画発表で驚かれた会員、我が意を得たりの人、さまざまの状

況でした。先ず、船体を作り、第一改装、第二次改装、または最終時の英姿、様々なプランが

生れて来ます。

このキットで以て念願であった１隻の戦艦の新造時より最終時迄を再現したい、これが可能

となりました。の連絡もあり。

このキットで日本戦艦８隻が製作出来る事は画期的なものです。

| 特別限定価格 | 1隻 ￥10,000− | 送料￥３００− |

内容、木甲板表現のカラーコピー　　2枚

菊華紋章（金メッキ仕上）

５００分の１図面

An advertisement in a Japanese warship modelling club magazine for Fuji-Art Model's kit of the HIJMS *Kongo* in 1/500 scale.

After the initial development of plastic model kits in Japan and the move to scales larger than 1/700, kits from other manufacturers began to appear. Bandai of Japan produced a kit of *Haruna*, and possibly the rest of the class, in 1/600 scale. This kit was toy-like and quite crude, which may be the reason why production was short; it is certainly very rare and hard to find.

Sometime in the late 1980s, or the early 1990s, a long standing Japanese company by the name of Fuji-Art, a producer of the highest quality drawings of Imperial Japanese Navy vessels, brass weapons and fittings in 1/500, 1/200 and 1/100 scales, began to produce kits in 1/500 scale.

These kits were considered 'craftsmen kits', in that the modeller received the primary components, plus weapons and fittings. Many of the finer details on the hull, superstructure and funnels were to be scratch built by the modeller. The larger components of these kits were cast in polyurethane resin, while the finer parts like weapons and fittings were investment cast brass. This type of kit had a short run, producing may be a hundred kits in total, making them quite rare and difficult to obtain.

HIJMS *Hiei* 1942 Fuji-Art Model

An image of a finished model of the *Kongo*, built from a Fuji-Art Model kit in 1/500 scale.

1/450 SCALE

Fujimi of Japan manufactured kits of the *Kongo* class battleships in 1/450 scale, beginning in 1977. They were semi-toy-like, but not too bad in accuracy. These were motorised, but could be built as a static display model. The hull was divided at the waterline, which was a good thing because the lower hull was not very accurate. The kit came with moulded-on life lines (railings), which could be removed without too much trouble. There were numerous inaccuracies in all portions of the superstructure, so extensive reworking of these areas was neccessary for at least some level of authenticity. The aircraft handling deck would need to be re-built, as the kit had it covered with wood and not the correct linoleum decking. The weapons and fittings could be re-worked, but some, like the 127mm twin AA mounts, needed a lot of additional attention.

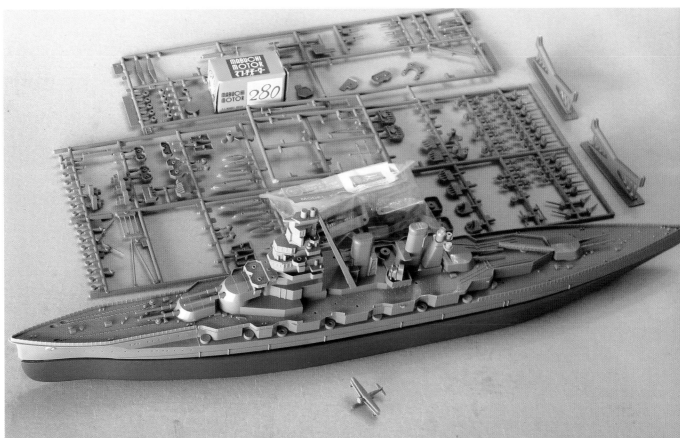

1/350 SCALE

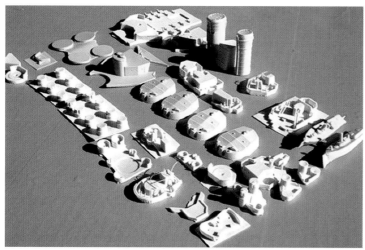

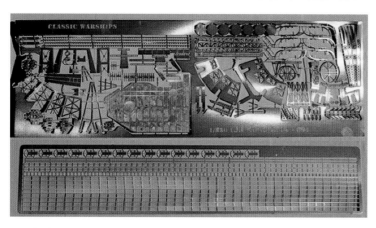

The first manufactured kit of any of the *Kongo* class battleships in 1/350 scale was produced by myself under the Classic Warships name in the USA. This 1/350 kit of the HIJMS *Kirishima*, in her 1942 configuration, was released in the late 1990s. I used the Fuji-Art drawings, then and I think still the most accurate available, to design the mould making pattern. This kit was and still is called a 'resin kit', but a more precise term would be 'multi-media kit', as it is made up of resin, white metal and photo-etch brass components. The design of this kit was quite difficult in my attempt to achieve the most accurate model possible. This made the kit construction a challenge to modellers, but the end result was always the same: the finished model looked like a photograph of the actual vessel. Construction of a resin kit is very different from assembling a plastic kit, so building a kit of this magnitude is not recommended for beginners. There is a good deal of clean-up and preparatory work with a resin kit, as well as a need for extreme dexterity when working with the hundreds of photo-etched brass detail parts. In 2005 I sold the model manufacturing portion of Classic Warships to Midship Models, which has a partnership with Yankee Modelworks and that is the brand name that the 1/350 *Kirishima* kit is now sold under. Until the 1/350 HIJMS *Nagato* offering by Hasegawa of Japan in 2007, this 1/350 *Kirishima* kit was the only other IJN battleship model in that scale, other than the *Yamato* class, offered world wide.

1/350 SCALE

Fujimi of Japan has, at the time of this publication, just released a 1/350 plastic model kit of HIJMS *Kongo* in her 1944 configuration. From the looks of the parts that come in the kit, it appears to be quite accurate and designed from the latest available documentation. Judging by the photographs of the parts trees and built-up corporate display models, the finesse of the detail on this model kit looks very promising. Fujimi has also just announced a 1/350 HIJMS *Haruna* in her 1944 fit as their next release. These new 1/350 scale kits will be a welcome addition to the range of IJN battleships, which have been confined to a very limited number in plastic and resin since the older Tamiya *Yamato* class released in the 1980s. Also, Aoshima of Japan has announced a 1/350 *Kongo* as well!

Kongo

Kongo

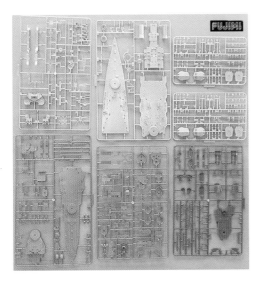

Haruna

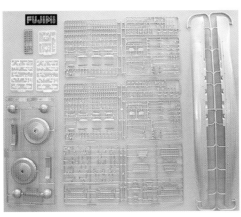

Haruna

Model Detail Accessories

There is a vast amount of detail accessories available to up-grade, or even convert kits to another version of the same vessel, or sistership. In fact, there are so many detail sets available, and becoming available, that this market is expanding at a dramatic rate. The quality of the products coming out is outstanding and each one is getting better with every new release. For contact information on any of the below mentioned companies, see the web site list on page 64 in the back of this book.

1/700, 1/500, 1/350 & 1/200 SCALE

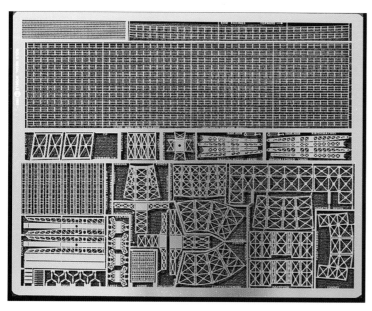

For the IJN *Kongo* class battleship, Gold Medal Models from the USA, the oldest and first model kit photo-etcher in the world, offers many sets of photo-etch in 1/700 to 1/200 scale that can be used to add extra details. Items included are anchors, hose and rope reels, ladders, ship's doors, and even decals for aircraft and flags. A generic IJN BB set in 1/700, pictured here, contains many items needed to up-grade the detail, or add more, for all of the *Kongo*s. Using GMM detail sets will vastly improve the look and detail of any model. Most highly recommended.

1/700 SCALE

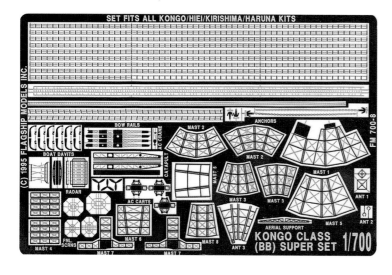

Flagship Models from the USA has produced a dedicated set of relief-etched photo-etch brass for the *Kongo* class battleships since the newer Hasegawa plastic kits came out in 1993. This set contains all the necessary basic detail items needed like catapults, anchors and chain, ladders and life lines, but also class specific items like the searchlight towers, radar antenna, and funnel grills. The design of the parts is good and the instructions are easy to follow while working with these small and delicate parts. This detail set will make a big difference to the look of any of the Hasegawa *Kongo* kits.

1/700, 1/500, 1/350 & 1/200 SCALE

Tom's Modelworks from the USA has an extensive line of photo-etch detail items for the IJN in 1/700, 1/500, 1/350 and 1/200 scales. Items range from ship's doors, pictured here, to anchors, cable reels, an IJN battleship set in 1/700, life lines, portholes in 1/350 and others. Another highly recommended product!

1/700, 1/450 & 1/350 SCALE

Eduard from the Czech Republic is a world leader in quality photo-etch products. They produce a number of different items for the IJN that relate to the *Kongo* class, including a dedicated set for the *Kirishima*, pictured here. Some of the other products they manufacture are pre-painted naval figures, miscellaneous IJN details, life lines, including a set in 1/450 that would work well with the Fujimi kit in that scale. Any and all of their product line is highly recommended.

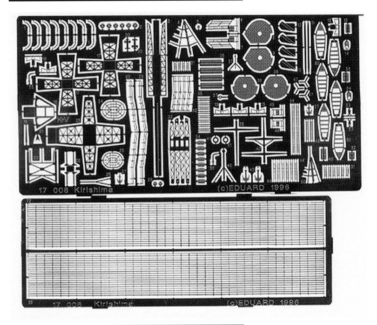

1/700, 1/500 & 1/350 SCALE

White Ensign Models from the United Kingdom produces a range of photo-etch detail parts for the IJN in three scales that all are dedicated to improving plastic kits. Items included are light AA weapons, pictured here in 1/350, doors & hatches, cable reels and life lines. This product line is amongst the best in the world, with some amazing levels of detail, and not for beginners! Highly recommended.

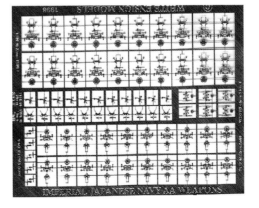

1/700 & 1/350 SCALE

Lion Roar of China has come on strong in just the last few years and has made great strides in their product line. They are currently producing over twenty-five sets of detail accessories in 1/700 scale and five in 1/350 scale that can be used to upgrade any of the *Kongo* class battleships. The upper image to the left is of their set for the

Hasegawa HIJMS *Nagato* and is shown to illustrate the level of detail their product provides. With the introduction of the new Fujimi and Aoshima *Kongo* kits, there is sure to be a dedicated set for them. The range and quality of product from this manufacturer is stunning, and highly recommended.

1/700 & 1/350 SCALE

The products of Voyager model, from China, are simply stunning. It is absolutely amazing how they are able to obtain the level of detail for their model accessories. Their products are made with the latest computer controlled machining and mould making technology. They produce a large array of detail sets in both 1/700 and 1/350 that are some of the best in the world. Within their product lines, there are many that can be used on any of the *Kongo* class battleships in both above mentioned scales. The item at top left is a 1/350 twin 127mm AA mount, the lower left image is of the IJN catapult in 1/700 and the image below is of their 1/700 triple 25mm mount. Accuracy in their product is good and the finesse of the detail is superb. They also produce resin cast ship's boats. Most highly recommended!

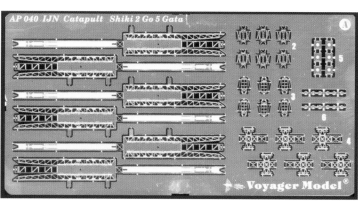

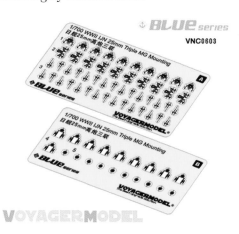

1/350 SCALE

Veteran Models of Hong Kong is absolutely the most amazing 1/350 model accessory company that this author was able to find. Their use of computer aided mould design has paid tangible dividends. As we can see by the sample images of their offerings pictured here on this page, Veteran Models produces some of the best detail items on the market today. All of the examples pictured here are applicable to any of the four of the *Kongo* class battleships. At first glance, the products in these images could easily be taken for detail accesories in 1/100scale: but no, these really are available in 1/350 in this level of finesse. As the success of their sales increases, we will, no doubt, see a lot more of this astounding output from this company in the future. It could not be more highly recommended.

IJN 6CM, 8CM, 12CM BINOCULAR SETS(WITH VOICE PIPES)

ITEM NO	VTW35032	6cm Binocular x 10 12cm Binocular x20
SCALE	1/350	Voice Pipe x 40 8cm Binocular x20
		Binocular with Signal Lamp x 4
		110cm Serach Light Controller x4
		Binocular with Infra-Red Message Transmitter x4

VETERAN MODELS WE BRIING YOU REAL SHIPS

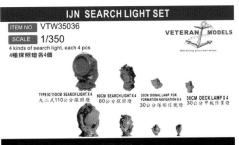

IJN SEARCH LIGHT SET

| ITEM NO | VTW35036 |
| SCALE | 1/350 |

4 kinds of search light, each 4 pcs
4種探照燈各4個

TYPE 92 110CM SEARCH LIGHT X 4　60CM SEARCH LIGHT X 4　30CM SIGNAL LAMP FOR FORMATION NAVIGATION X4　30CM DECK LAMP X 4
九二式110公分探照燈　60公分探照燈　30公分隊形信號燈　30公分甲板作業燈

VETERAN MODELS WE BRING YOU REAL SHIPS

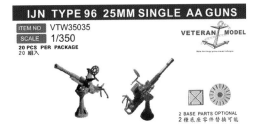

IJN TYPE 96 25MM SINGLE AA GUNS

| ITEM NO | VTW35035 |
| SCALE | 1/350 |

20 PCS PER PACKAGE
20 組入

2 BASE PARTS OPTIONAL
2 種底座零件替換可能

VETERAN MODELS WE BRING YOU REAL SHIPS

IJN TYPE 96 25MM TWIN AA GUNS

| ITEM NO | VTW35034 |
| SCALE | 1/350 |

10 PCS PER PACKAGE
10 組入

VETERAN MODELS WE BRING YOU REAL SHIPS

TYPE 89 12.7CM 40CAL AA GUNS

| ITEM NO | VTW35031 | (Fuse Second Controller |
| SCALE | 1/350 | & Brass Barrels included) |

4PCS PER PACKAGE

VETERAN MODELS WE BRIING YOU REAL SHIPS

IJN TYPE 96 25MM TRIPLE AA GUNS

| ITEM NO | VTW35033 |
| SCALE | 1/350 |

10 PCS PER PACKAGE
10 組入

We bring you real ships

VETERAN MODELS WE BRING YOU REAL SHIPS

1/350 SCALE

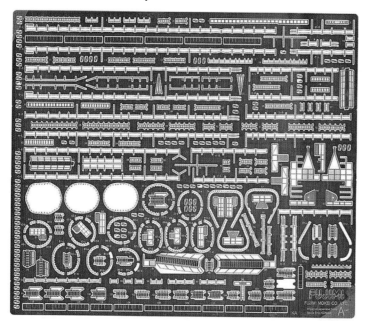

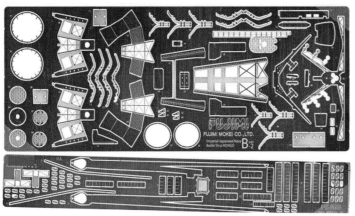

Fujimi of Japan has become aware of the large demand for after-market detail accessories and is making them for their own kits. Why not? The quality of the brass detail parts is outstanding. Accuracy is really high, as well as having relief-etched brass. The number of parts in each set is impressive. The addition of these sets will enable one to construct an absolute museum piece with the utmost in detail. Pictured here are all four sets of extra detail items, not including the life lines, as well as the turned brass main gun barrels. This author suspects that Fujimi will be producing the other two (*Hiei* and *Kirishima*) vessels of this class, and therefore also releasing further detail sets. These sets are highly recommended.

Note: There are other small Japanese companies producing further detail parts, like the 6in secondary gun barrels, with blast bags, by Fukuya, available through Hobby Link Japan.

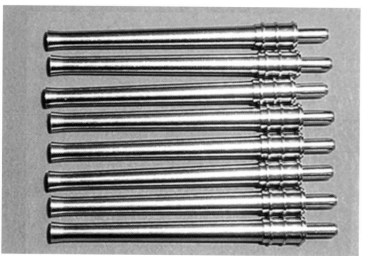

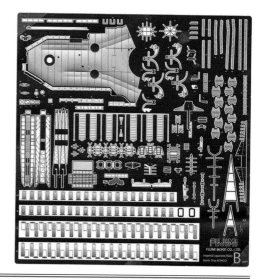

1/350 SCALE

Just found! A real wood replacement scale deck for the new 1/350 *Kongo* kits! Shinsengumi is the company name, from Japan, available through Hobby Link Japan.

Modelmakers' Showcase

The completed models in this section of the book represent the top end of the skills range. They were constructed either by advanced kit builders or highly proficient scratch builders. All of the examples here have had numerous additional details added by the builders and represent all four of the *Kongo* class battleships from the Imperial Japanese Navy.

Classic Warships /
Yankee Modelworks
1/350 scale HIJMS
Kirishima

Hasegawa
1/350 scale
HIJMS *Hiei*

Fujimi
1/350 scale
HIJMS *Kongo*

HIJMS *KIRISHIMA* 1/350 scale   by COL C PARKER

Col C Parker, US Army (Ret), resident in the Washington, DC area, Maryland, USA, has constructed the HIJMS *Kirishima* from the old Classic Warships, now Yankee Modelworks kit 'out of the box,' with some minor details scratch built. The finished model appears almost as if it were the original vessel in historic photographs. That is a goal of all model builders, but achieved by very few. Much research was done during the construction phase to ensure an accurate representation of this warship. One of the characteristic features of IJN warships in WWII commonly missed by model builders is

the weathered look of vessels of that navy. Col Parker has used several washes of paint over this model to give it a correct heavy weathered appearance. This model represents *Kirishima* about 1942, at the time of her loss in the naval battles of Guadalcanal.

In these views of the primary superstructure, one can see the amount of rigging detail achieved by this builder. A common shortcoming of many models is insufficient or inaccurate rigging, but this is such a noticeable feature that it is worth making a special effort, as was done here. Note the rigging of the ship's boats, as well

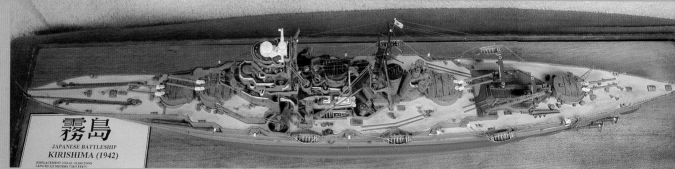

霧島

JAPANESE BATTLESHIP
KIRISHIMA (1942)
DISPLACEMENT 1935-42: 32,460 TONS
LENGTH 222 METERS (728.5 FEET)

as their painting. Compare with those on page 44 for a pre-war version.

The construction and painting of a Second World War capital ship's aircraft is an important element in the construction of a model of this quality. They need to be done correctly, because they are a major focal point of a model. Note the orientation of the propellers in the image on page 35. They are correct. This is a feature that is often inaccurately portrayed on many models.

HIJMS *KONGO* 1/48 scale

VICKERS LTD

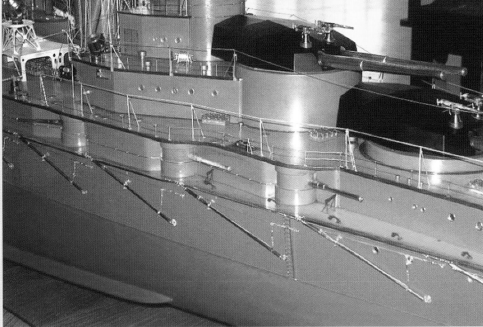

The official Vickers builders' model, now displayed at The Dock Museum, Barrow in Furness, UK.

HIJMS *KONGO* 1/350 scale

by FUJIMI MOKEI

Fujimi Models of Japan has just released their plastic model kit of the HIJMS *Kongo* in her 1944 configuration. At 25 inches in length, this is an impressive model. As we can see by these photos of an 'out of the box' build, the detail is very good and the accuracy of the kit is also very well done.

Some of the detail items like the supports for the searchlight platforms around the forward funnel are a little on the heavy side, but better than has been presented in the past on other kits. I am quite sure there will be an abundance of after-market detail products available in the very near future that will greatly enhance the already very good quality of this model kit.

By 1944 the Imperial Japanese Navy was running low on resources, one of which was paint. Their vessels were not maintained well, which also meant that you would see vessels with a significant amount of weathering. That would add a nice touch of realism to this magnificent model.

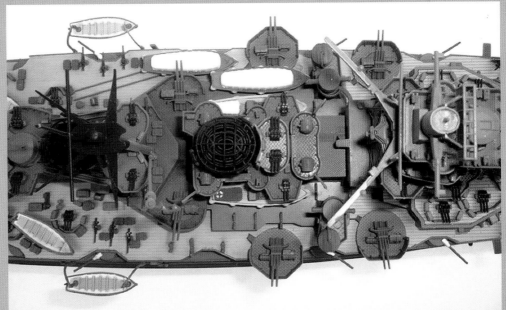

HIJMS *HIEI* 1/700 scale

by L MOSBAEK

HIJMS *Hiei*, by L Mosbaek in 1/700 scale. The starting point for this model was the Hasegawa kit, but it required an immense amount of scratch built corrections and details, as well as the addition of a multitude of photo-etch accessories. Mr Mosbaek has done a wonderful job of weathering this model, representing the wood decks very well. Note also the superb work on the ship's rigging, which is quite difficult in this scale.

HIJMS *HARUNA* 1/150 scale

by K OKAMOTO

This is one of the best built and detailed models of all *Kongo* class battleships, let alone *Haruna*, in the world. The level of detail is stunning to say the least. This model of the HIJMS *Haruna* represents her at the conclusion of her major reconstruction in September 1934.

Because of the intense concentration of detail and degree of accuracy in this model, Mr Okamoto is considered the leading authority on the *Haruna* and the other vessels of the *Kongo* class. As one can see by the images here of the bridge structure, this model was constructed in sub-assemblies. In fact, the sub-assemblies are constructed of sub-assemblies, due to the amazing level of fine detail to which this model was built.

The materials used in the construction of this model range through wood, plastics, brass rod, brass tubing and card stock. One must also realise that all items and components of this model are completely scratch built. There is not a source for fittings available in this scale. Only items like the thread that represents the rope and the chain for the anchor cable were available for purchase. Mr Okamoto built each and every

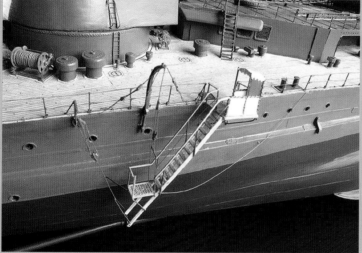

one of the remaining parts of this model himself.

Ship models such as this masterpiece are rare and, being privately owned, infrequently available for viewing. We are left with only photographs, which, I can tell you, do not do justice to models of this calibre. However, the one benefit to photos of a model like this is that they are a great reference tool, especially for those who build in a smaller scale.

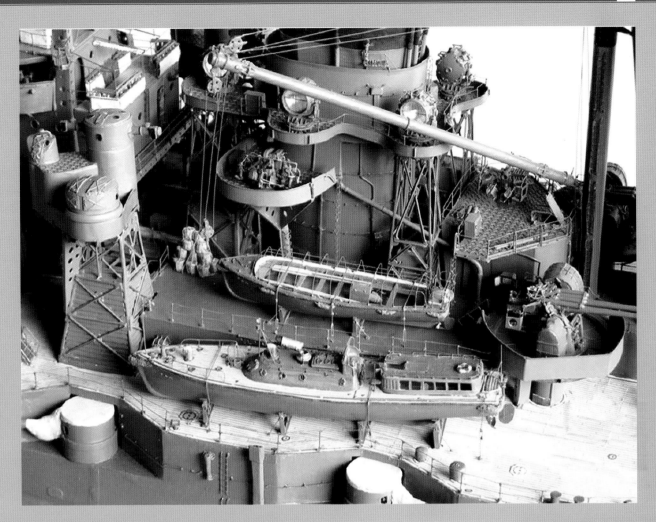

日本海軍 榛名

1/150

平成18年7月完成

HIJMS *HARUNA* 1/700 scale

by T KIMOTO

This 1944 version of HIJMS *Haruna* was constructed by Toshifumi Kimoto of Japan. Mr Kimoto used the Hasegawa kit as his project starting point. He used photo-etched details from several manufacturers, as well as some scratch built details. Many minor and some major corrections were also accomplished in the construction of this model. Note the covered port holes, photo-etched light AA mounts and the addition of the degaussing cable. The model is fully rigged, using drawings of the *Haruna* available from various vendors. See his web site, Vanguard Models, for ship modelling, listed on page 64.

HIJMS *Hiei* – 1942

Drawings provided by Model Art Co, Ltd.
Colorisation by Steve Wiper

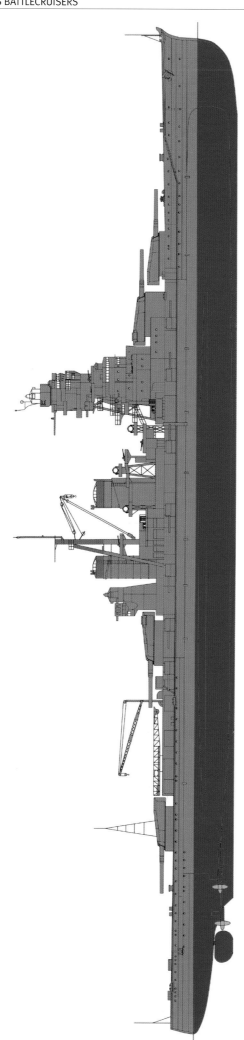

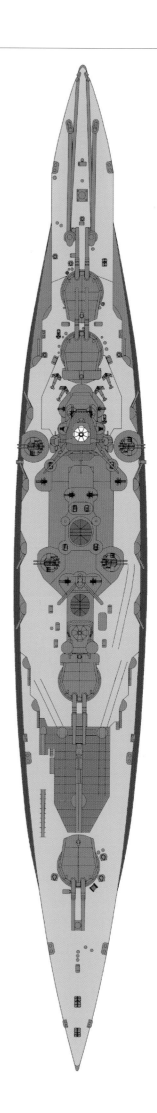

HIJMS *Kongo* – 1913

Drawings provided by Model Art Co, Ltd.

HIJMS *Haruna* – 1928

HIJMS *Hiei* – 1934

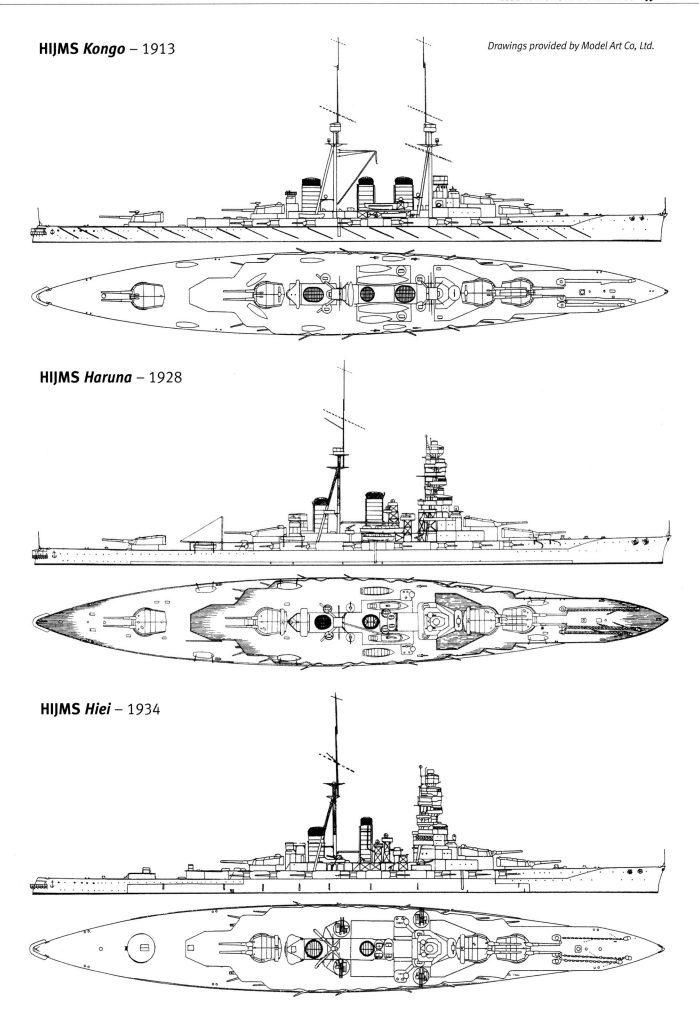

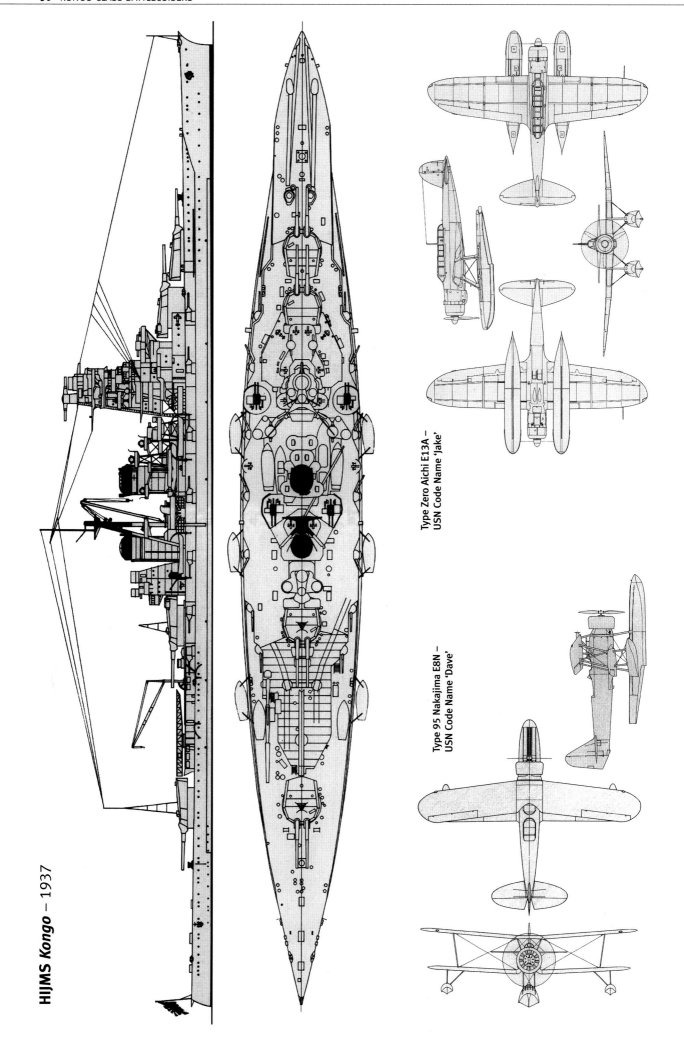

HIJMS *Kongo* – 1937

Type Zero Aichi E13A – USN Code Name 'Jake'

Type 95 Nakajima E8N – USN Code Name 'Dave'

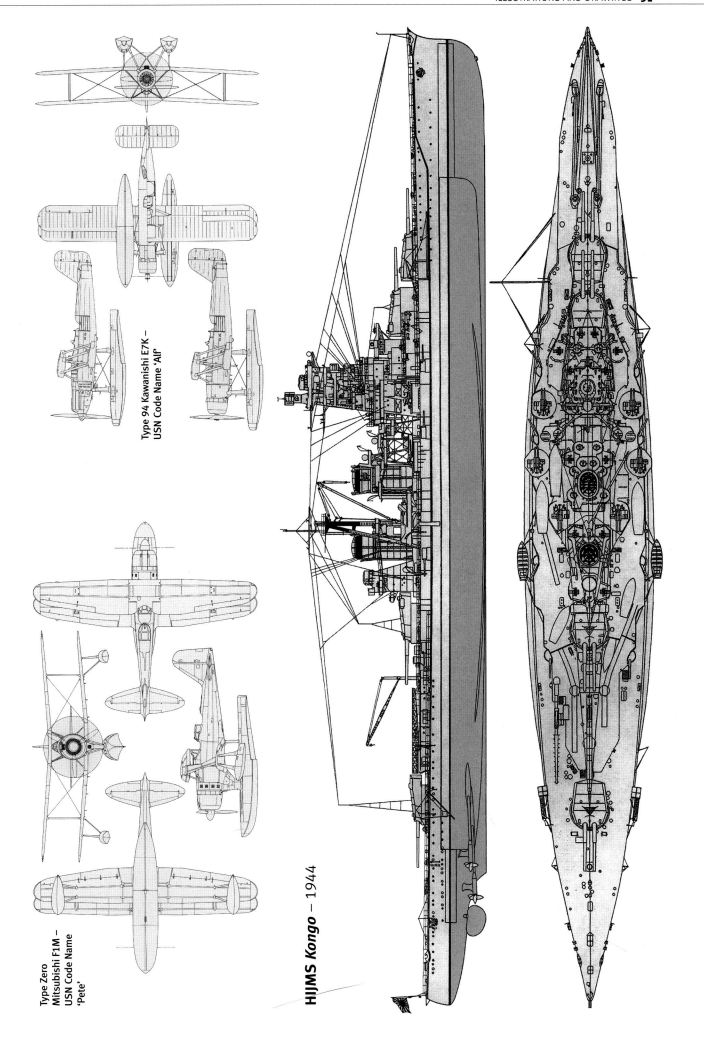

Type 94 Kawanishi E7K –
USN Code Name 'Alf'

Type Zero
Mitsubishi F1M –
USN Code Name
'Pete'

HIJMS *Kongo* – 1944

Drawings provided by Model Art Co, Ltd.

HIJMS *Hiei* – 1942

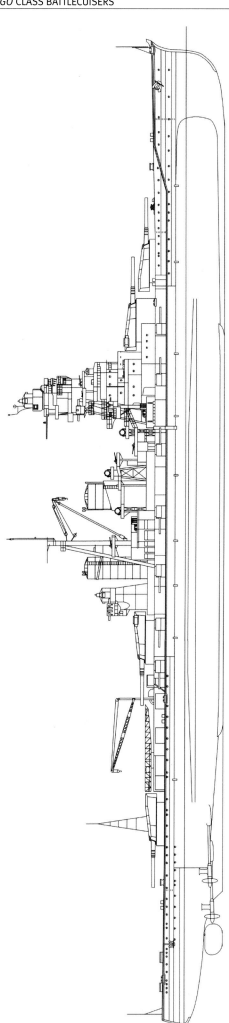

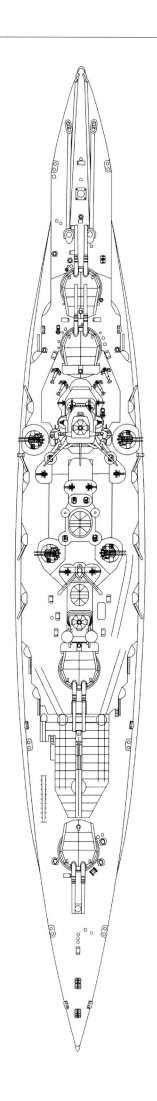

Drawings provided by Model Art Co, Ltd.

HIJMS *Kirishima* – 1941

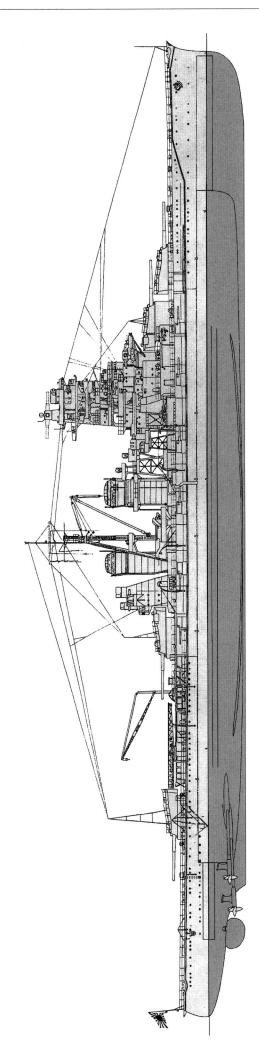

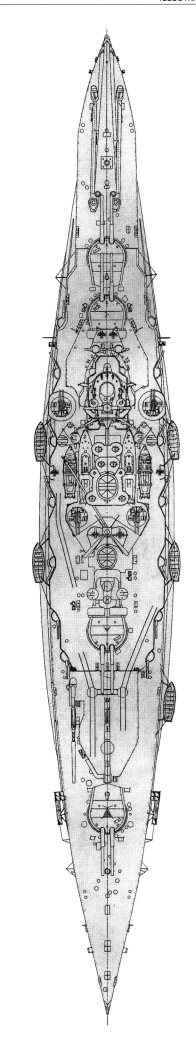

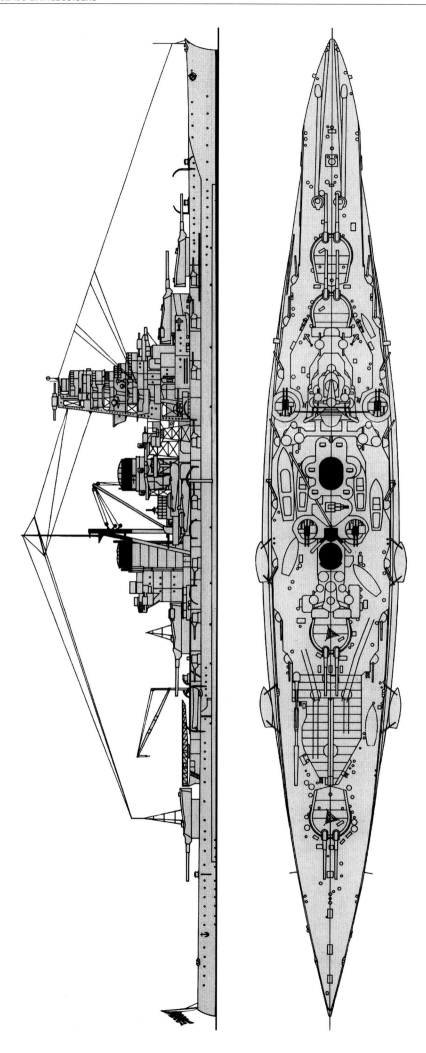

Drawings provided by Model Art Co., Ltd.

HIJMS *Haruna* – 1937

Drawings provided by Model Art Co, Ltd.

HIJMS *Haruna* – 1944

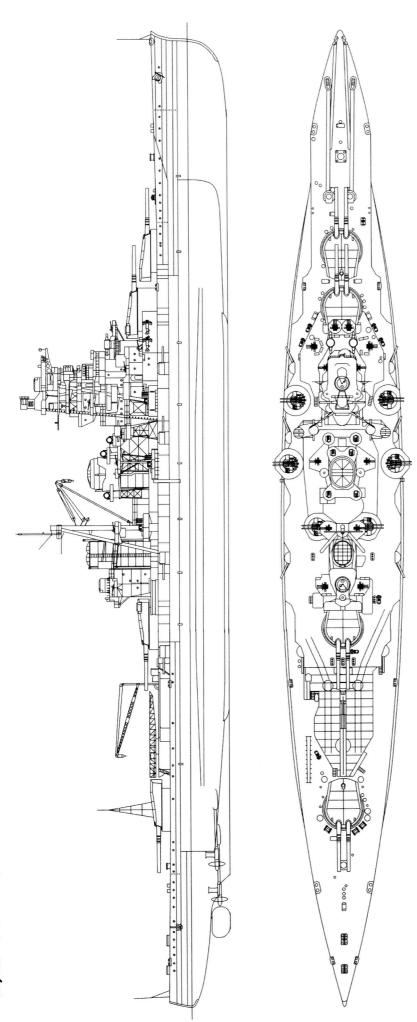

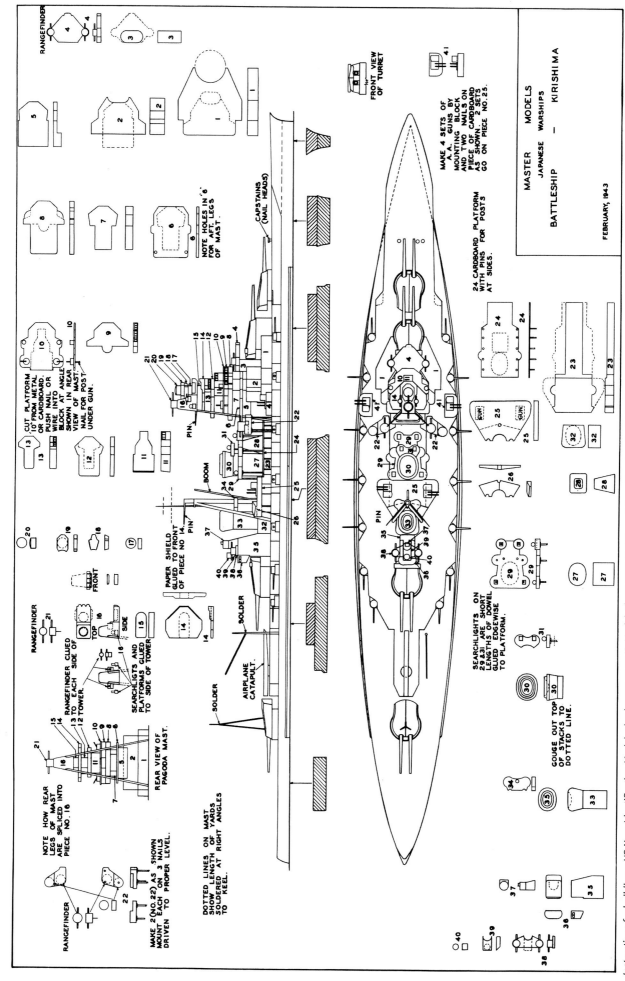

Instructions for building a US Navy Identification Model, also known as an ID Model. These were built to an International scale of 1/500

ONI 41-42

KONGO CLASS BB—1-4

DIVISION OF NAVAL INTELLIGENCE—IDENTIFICATION AND CHARACTERISTICS SECTION—NOVEMBER, 1942

HEIGHT OF OBSERVER

135	135
120	120
105	105
90	90
75	75
60	60
45	45
30	30
15	15

HORIZON BEYOND THE SHIP

SHIP BEYOND THE HORIZON

0

LENGTH—704' OA
BEAM— 95'
DRAFT— 27' 6" (NORMAL)

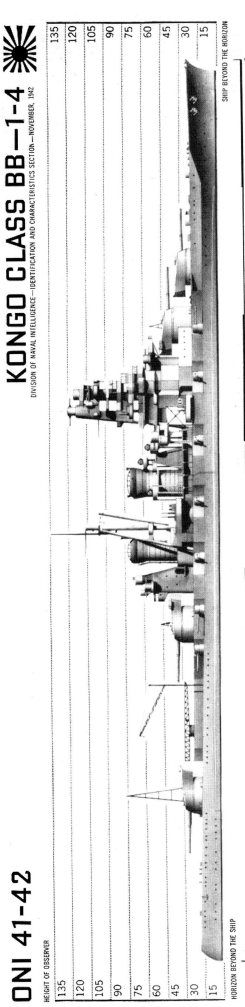

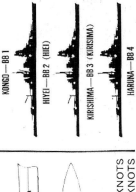

KONGO CLASS

KONGO—BB 1

HIYEI—BB 2 (HIEI)

KIRISHIMA—BB 3 (KIRISIMA)

HARUNA—BB 4

PROPULSION

DES HP— 78,000   DES SPEED—26 KNOTS
ENDURANCE—3,500 @ 26 KNOTS   12,600 @ 12 KNOTS

DISPLACEMENT—29,300 TONS (STANDARD)—30,500 TONS (NORMAL)

ARMAMENT

	MAX. ELEV.	RANGE
8–14" (45)	30°	30,000 YD.
14–6" (50) CASEMATES	25°	19,000 YD.
8–5" AA TWIN MOUNTS	85°	18,000 YD.

1 CATAPULT, 3 SCOUT OBSERVATION
NOTE: HIYEI, ONCE DEMILITARIZED; MAY HAVE WEAKER
ORDNANCE.

PROTECTION

BELT—   6"–8" WITH 3" ENDS
TURRETS—   9"–10"
BARBETTES—   10"
CONNING TOWER—10"
DECK—   2¾"–4"; 7" OVER VITALS

DENSITY OF FIRE
MAIN BATTERY

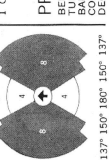

35° 28° 28° 35°
0°

137° 150° 180° 150° 137°

The page for the *Kongo* class from the official wartime USN recognition manual

The image above is a rare aerial view of the aircraft handling deck of *Hiei*, taken about early 1940.

Below is a famous photo of *Kirishima*, 27 April 1939, in Sukumo Bay, Japan.

HIJMS *Hiei* at full power during her machinery trials at the conclusion of her major reconstruction, 5 December 1939. She received a reconstruction similar to that of her sisterships, but the bridge structure was different, being in essence a prototype that would evolve into that used on *Yamato*.

Above is *Kongo* in waters off Japan during a five-day series of fleet manouevres, 19-23 May 1942. Note the Hinomaru on canvas tied to the top of main gun turrets 2 and 4. Also, the foretop rangefinders were painted bright white as another identification marking for IJN recognition.

Above is another rare view of the aircraft handling deck of a *Kongo* class battleship, this one of *Kirishima*, about 1940.

Below is a photograph of *Hiei* at sea on the same manouevres as *Kongo* in the image at the top of this page.

Opposite: Four photographs of the *Kongo* in early 1942. In both of the top images on this page, the use of the stuffed canvas for splinter protection can be seen. The lower left image of *Kongo*'s fore deck is a good view of the tops of the turrets and their additional armour plates that were added in her last major overhaul. The image below of the after side of *Kongo*'s bridge shows some of the massive bracing on the underside of the different platforms. Note that the director is barely visible because is was painted white for air recognition.

Right: A view of the fore deck of *Hiei*, about 1942. Note the high elevation of her main guns. This extended her firing range significantly.

The four photos below are the last known images of the IJN battleship *Hiei*. In these photos she was under attack from USAAF B-17s at about 8000ft, that dropped fifty-six 500lb bombs. *Hiei* began to manouevre to avoid the attack, but was struck by at least one bomb. In these photographs her bridge appears to be on fire. She was off Savo Island at that time, trying in the early pre-dawn darkness to repair some of the severe damage received during the first naval Battle of Guadalcanal.

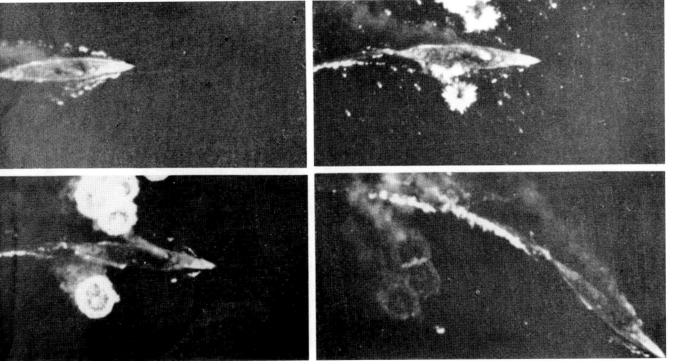

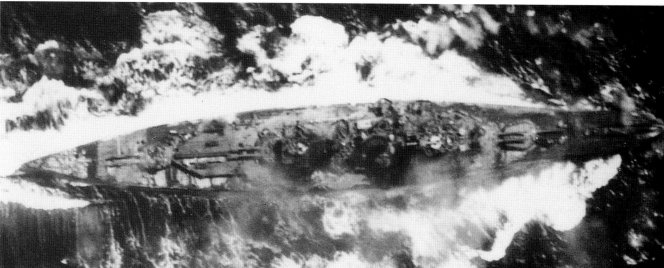

Haruna under attack from high altitude USAAF bombers on 26 October 1944, one day after the defeat of the IJN at the Battle off Samar. She is saling through through Tablas Strait, off Panay Island, to the IJN anchorage at Brunei. During this attack by USAAF B-24 bombers, no hits were scored on *Haruna*, which manouevred wildly to avoid 500lb bombs dropped from approximately 14,000ft. Many of the additional 25mm AA mounts are visible in this image.

Both of these images are of *Haruna* under attack by aircraft from the US Navy carriers USS *Wasp* (CV-18) and USS *Shangri-La* (CV-38). This attack was on 28 July 1945, when *Haruna* was hit by at least six 500lb bombs, causing her to sink in the shallow water in which she was anchored.

All of the images on this page are of HIJMS *Haruna*, taken from September to October 1945, during a survey by the US Naval Technical Mission to Japan of the remnants of the Imperial Japanese Navy after the end of hostilities. The extent of bomb damage to *Haruna* is seen here. She sank after the attacks at the end of July 1945. Most of the light anti-aircraft weapons were moved ashore in an effort to better protect the vessel, to no avail against an overwhelming attack by US Navy carrier based aircraft.

Additional References

Campbell, John, *Naval Weapons of World War Two*, Conway Maritime Press Ltd, London, 1985.

Chihaya, Masataka & Abe, Yasuo, *IJN Kongo: Battleship 1912-1944* (Warship Profile 12), Profile Publications, Windsor 1971.

Dull, Paul S., *Battle History of the Imperial Japanese Navy (1941-1945)*, Naval Institute Press, Annapolis, 1978.

Fitzsimons, Bernard, *Weapons and Warfare – The Illustrated Encyclopedia of 20th Century*, Vol. 1 through 24, Purnell & Sons Ltd, New York, 1967.

Friedman, Norman, *Naval Radar*, Conway Maritime Press Ltd, London, 1981.

Gardiner, Robert, *Conway's – All The World's Fighting Ships – 1906-1921*, Naval Institute Press, Annapolis, 1980.

Gardiner, Robert, *Conway's – All The World's Fighting Ships – 1922-1946*, Naval Institute Press, Annapolis, 1980.

Government Printing Office, *U. S. Stategic Bombing Survey – Pacific War*, GPO, Washington, DC, 1946.

Jentshura, Hansgeorg, Jung, Dieter & Mickel, Peter, *Warships of the Imperial Japanese Navy 1869-1945*, Arms & Armour Press, London 1977

Morrison, Samuel Eliot, *History of US Naval Operations in WWII*, Vol. 1 through 15, Little Brown & Co, Boston, 1951.

Naval Intelligence, US Division of, *The Japanese Navy in World War II*, Proceedings 1952-1958, Naval Institute Press, Annapolis, 1969

Naval Intelligence, US Division of, *Japanese Naval Vessels of WWII*, ONI 41-42, Naval Institute Press, Annapolis, 1987.

WARSHIP MODELLING WEBSITES, MANUFACTURERS & SUPPLIERS

www.aeronautic.dk
www.alnavco.com
www.aoshima-bk.co.jp
www.chamame29.web.fc2.com
www.combinedfleet.com
www.cybermodeler.com
www.eduard.cz
www.flagshipmodels.com
www.fujimimokei.com
www.gakken.co.jp
www.ghqmodels.com
www.goldmm.com
www.hasegawa-model.co.jp
www.h3.dion.ne.jp/~mokei/
www.jtw.zaq.ne.jp/wakamo/
www.lionroar.net
www.modelart.jp
www.ModelShip.info/Minekaze
www.modelships.info/veteranmodels
www.modelwarships.com
www.navis-neptun.de
www.pacificfront.com
www.steelnavy.com
www.tomsmodelworks.com
http://homepage2.nifty.com/
    vanguard/intro/main2.htm
www.voyagermodel.com
www.warshipmodelsunderway.com
www.whiteensignmodels.com
www.yankeemodelworks.com

WARSHIP RESEARCH WEBSITES

www.classicwarships.com
www.combinedfleet.com
www.history.navy.mil

ACKNOWLEDGEMENTS

Assistance -
Don S. Montgomery
Dan Kaplan
Ron Smith
Photography -
Authors Collection
US National Archives
US Naval Historical Center
Drawings -
Authors Collection
Model Art Publications